Art is never finished, only abandoned.
LEONARDO DA VINCI

If you always do what you always did— you'll always get what you always got.
UNKNOWN

If I create from the heart, nearly everything works; if from the head, almost nothing.
MARC CHAGALL

It is only by drawing often, drawing everything, drawing incessantly, that one fine day
you discover to your surprise that you have rendered something in its true character.
CAMILLE PISSARO

Art washes away from the soul the dust of everyday life.
PABLO PICASSO

The job of the artist is always to deepen the mystery.
FRANCIS BACON

To practice any art, no matter how well or badly, is a way to make your soul grow. So do it.
KURT VONNEGUT

Those who do not want to imitate anything, produce nothing.
SALVADOR DALI

Drawing is still basically the same as it has been since prehistoric times.
It brings together man and the world. It lives through magic.
KEITH HARING

Life inspires me to paint. Painting inspires me to paint.
DION ARCHIBALD

To create one's own world takes courage.
GEORGIA O'KEEFFE

Art is not what you see, but what you make others see.
EDGAR DEGAS

The whole culture is telling you to hurry, while the art tells you to take your time. Always listen to the art.
JUNOT DIAZ

In art, the hand can never execute anything higher than the heart can imagine.
RALPH WALDO EMERSON

Art enables us to find ourselves and lose ourselves at the same time.
THOMAS MERTON

The object of art is not to reproduce reality, but to create a reality of the same intensity.
ALBERTO GIACOMETTI

Whether you succeed or not is irrelevant, there is no such thing.
Making your unknown known is the important thing.
GEORGIA O'KEEFFE

We all have the ability... we just don't all have the courage to follow our dreams and to follow the signs.
PAULO COELHO

One eye sees, the other feels.
PAUL KLEE

Discipline in art is a fundamental struggle to understand oneself, as much as to understand what one is drawing.
HENRY MOORE

Dwell on the beauty of life. Watch the stars, and see yourself running with them.
MARCUS AURELIUS

The artist is a receptacle for emotions that come from all over the place: from the sky,
from the earth, from a scrap of paper, from a passing shape, from a spider's web.
PABLO PICASSO

Many are they who have a taste and love for drawing, but no talent; and this will be
discernible in boys who are not diligent and never finish their drawings with shading.
LEONARDO DA VINCI

Inspiration comes of working every day.
CHARLES BAUDELAIRE

Do not fear mistakes—there are none.
MILES DAVIS

Painting is poetry that is seen rather than felt, and poetry is painting that is felt rather than seen.
LEONARDO DA VINCI

Don't think about making art, just get it done. Let everyone else decide if it's good or bad,
whether they love it or hate it. While they are deciding, make even more art.
ANDY WARHOL

If you can dream it, you can achieve it.
ZIG ZIGLAR

A work of art which did not begin in emotion is not art.
PAUL CEZANNE

The artist must raise the cup of his vision aloft to the gods in the high hope
that they will pour into it the sweet mellow wine of inspiration.
PAUL BRUNTON

Art doesn't have to be pretty. It has to be meaningful.
DUANE HANSON

Have no fear of perfection, you'll never reach it.
SALVADOR DALI

Creativity is allowing yourself to make mistakes. Art is knowing which ones to keep.
SCOTT ADAMS

Inspiration is a byproduct of discipline... simply getting up everyday and planning,
plotting, sketching, setting up or actually applying paint to a painting.
BEVERLY CLARIDGE

The most beautiful experience we can have is the mysterious—the fundamental
emotion which stands at the cradle of true art and true science.
ALBERT EINSTEIN

The position of the artist is humble. He is essentially a channel.
PIET MONDRIAN

The longer you look at an object, the more abstract it becomes, and, ironically, the more real.
LUCIAN FREUD

To draw, you must close your eyes and sing.
PABLO PICASSO

Colour is my day-long obsession, joy and torment.
CLAUDE MONET

Go and make interesting mistakes, make amazing mistakes, make glorious and fantastic mistakes.
Break rules. Leave the world more interesting for your being here. Make. Good. Art.
NEIL GAIMAN

My attitude towards drawing is not necessarily about drawing. It's about making the
best kind of image I can make, it's about talking as clearly as I can.
JIM DINE

Inspiration may be a form of superconsciousness, or perhaps of subconsciousness—
I wouldn't know. But I am sure it is the antithesis of self-consciousness.
AARON COPLAND

Do not fail, as you go on, to draw something every day, for no matter
how little it is, it will be well worthwhile, and it will do you a world of good.
CENNINO CENNINI

Everything you can imagine is real.
PABLO PICASSO

If you ask me what I came to do in this world, I, an artist, will answer you: I am here to live out loud.
ÉMILE ZOLA

The only time I feel alive is when I'm painting.
VINCENT VAN GOGH

The main thing is to be moved, to love, to hope, to tremble, to live.
AUGUSTE RODIN

I found I could say things with color and shapes that I couldn't say any other way—things I had no words for.
GEORGIA O'KEEFFE

There is no must in art because art is free.
WASSILY KANDINSKY

The holy grail is to spend less time making the picture than it takes people to look at it.
BANKSY

Art is the only way to run away without leaving home.
TWYLA THARP

You might as well ask an artist to explain his art, or ask a poet to explain his poem.
It defeats the purpose. The meaning is only clear thorough the search.
RICK RIORDAN

An artist cannot fail; it is a success to be one.
CHARLES HORTON COOLEY

Art is not a thing, it is a way.
ELBERT HUBBARD

The superior man is distressed by the limitations of his ability; he is not
distressed by the fact that men do not recognize the ability that he has.
CONFUCIUS

Paint the flying spirit of the bird rather than its feathers.
ROBERT HENRI

An artist needs to take many tiny baby steps to achieve and maintain quality and continuity.
ELIZABETH AZZOLINA

Art is when you hear a knocking from your soul—and you answer.
TERRI GUILLEMETS

Art reaches its greatest peak when devoid of self-consciousness. Freedom discovers man the moment he loses concern over what impression he is making or about to make.
BRUCE LEE

You can't do sketches enough. Sketch everything and keep your curiosity fresh.
JOHN SINGER SARGENT

I dream my painting and I paint my dream.
VINCENT VAN GOGH

Beauty is the illumination of your soul.
JOHN O'DONOHUE

Art attracts us only by what it reveals of our most secret self.
JEAN-LUC GODARD

It is good to love many things, for therein lies the true strength, and whosoever loves much
performs much, and can accomplish much, and what is done in love is well done.
VINCENT VAN GOGH

The day is coming when a single carrot, freshly observed, will set off a revolution.
PAUL CEZANNE

When it is working, you completely go into another place, you're tapping into things that are
totally universal, completely beyond your ego and your own self. That's what it's all about.
KEITH HARING

Learn the rules like a pro, so you can break them like an artist.
PABLO PICASSO

The aim of art is to represent not the outward appearance of things, but their inward significance.
ARISTOTLE

To send light into the darkness of men's hearts—such is the duty of the artist.
ROBERT SCHUMANN

The reason that art (writing, engaging, and all of it) is valuable is precisely why I can't tell you how to do it.
If there were a map, there'd be no art, because art is the act of navigating without a map.
SETH GODIN

Practice random beauty and senseless acts of love.
ANONYMOUS

About two-thirds of the effort that goes towards the execution
of a painting can, I am sure, be attributed to observation.
LIONEL AGGETT

Absent imagination and artistic vision, we are blind to the wonders of creation.
DAVID ALLIO

Often it is tiny fragments which either make a picture convincing or totally incidental.
SIMONE BINGEMER

Art is a lie that makes us realize truth.
PABLO PICASSO

It's through my artist's eyes that I see wonderful things in nature that I never saw before.
KATHY CONNELLY

Art and love are the same thing: It's the process of seeing yourself in things that are not you.
CHUCK KLOSTERMAN

The ability to simplify means to eliminate the unnecessary so that the necessary may speak.
HANS HOFMANN

Inspiration does exist but it must find you working.
PABLO PICASSO

Creativity is the voice of the spirit. One's art should be the extension of oneself.
MARITZA BURGOS

Be who you are and say what you feel because those who mind don't matter and those who matter don't mind.
DR. SEUSS

Drawing is the "bones" of art. You have to be able to walk before you can run.
DION ARCHIBALD

It took me four years to paint like Raphael, but a lifetime to paint like a child.
PABLO PICASSO

When you conquer negative attitudes of doubt and fear you conquer failure.
BRYAN ADAMS

Certain things catch your eye, but pursue only those that capture the heart.
ANCIENT INDIAN PROVERB

A law of composition: If it does not fit do not force it; it is not for it.
JACK BARTHOLOMEW

If I were called upon to define briefly the word Art, I should call it the reproduction
of what the senses perceive in nature, seen through the veil of the soul.
PAUL CEZANNE

The greatest art is to sit, and wait, and let it come.
YOGI BHAJAN

Every child is an artist. The problem is how to remain an artist once he grows up.
PABLO PICASSO

It's not what you look at that matters, it's what you see.
HENRY DAVID THOREAU

Everything has beauty, but not everyone can see.
CONFUCIUS

Trust in yourself. Your perceptions are often far more accurate than you are willing to believe.
CLAUDIA BLACK

Developing a composition is a creative process involving intuition and thinking more than following rules.
ALESSANDRA BITELLI

Practice by drawing things large, as if equal in representation and reality. In small drawings
Every large weakness is easily hidden; in the large, the smallest weakness is easily seen.
LEON BATTISTA ALBERTI

I invent nothing, I rediscover.
AUGUSTE RODIN

Affirm it, visualize it, and it will actualize itself.
UNKNOWN

Every day that you don't practice is a day you're getting worse.
AMY CHUA

All our dreams can come true if we have the courage to pursue them.
WALT DISNEY

Go confidently in the direction of your dreams. Live the life you have imagined.
HENRY DAVID THOREAU